# Why Set up an Escort Agency?

# Why Set up an Escort Agency?

### KARL CROSSFIELD

# CONTENTS

# 1

## WHY SET UP AN ESCORT AGENCY?

People often ask me: What was the best thing about running an escort agency? It's a question that could have a dozen answers, but for me, it is very simple. The best thing about running an escort agency is *the buzz*.

As the reader of this book, you probably share my entrepreneurial spirit and know exactly what I mean by *the buzz*. It's the feeling of speaking to a client over the phone at the end of their appointment and hearing how much they enjoyed their time with one of your escorts. It's the feeling of seeing your classy advert in the local newspaper or the excitement of counting the money at the end of the week.

My entrepreneurial spirit began as a 10-year-old in the 1970s, when I'd collect empty glass soda bottles from the local rugby club and haul them to the grocery shop. In those days, each empty bottle could be returned for a 2p deposit, and all profit went on big bags of brightly coloured sherbet!

On other occasions, whenever the travelling fayre came to town, I'd be ready and waiting for the moment they departed the following Sunday. The spot where each stall, booth or ride had stood was replaced with a dusty pile of recently swept trash, and within each would be several dropped coins just waiting to be found.

Whether dipping my fingers into a hard-earned bag of sherbet or running my hands through fairground litter in the hope of a coin, I felt *the buzz*. I've had many jobs over the years since, from key-cutting and cobbling to carpet-fitting and screen-printing. I've been an ice cream man, a park ranger, a land-train driver, and now—a writer! Still, nothing comes close to the excitement and success of setting up my own escort agency in 1998.

Before we go any further, there is of course one question that needs to be answered: What is an escort? A common misconception is that an escort is simply a code word for a prostitute, but the two are entirely different. An escort is a social companion for hire. A prostitute sells sexual services.

This book isn't about becoming a pimp or running a brothel. Under the Sexual Offences Act 2003, such practices are clearly proscribed and could land you with a hefty prison sentence. This is about something legal and ethical, and above all else, deeply meaningful.

The eye-catching companion at a business function, the charming plus-one at a wedding or party or the dinner date who makes time fly by and loneliness fly away: these are the moments a good escort can create, and they are moments worth paying for.

## FORMER ICE CREAM SELLER WHIPS UP TRADE AS ESCORT AGENCY

# Ice cream man Karl makes the hearts melt

Karl Crossfield: Helps lonely business people find companions. Photo: STEVE BOULD

**By Tahira Yaqoob**

WHEN business cooled for ice cream seller Karl Crossfield, he decided there was money to be made elsewhere – arranging escorts *for single men and women.*

Karl, from Stoke-on-Trent, set up his own escort agency advertising male and female companions for all occasions... and now business is booming.

In the seven weeks since he set up his new venture, he has signed 22 women and six men aged between 24 and 40 as escorts.

But getting rid of loneliness does not come cheap as Karl's escorts cost £40 an hour. Karl keeps profiles of all his escorts and matches them up to clients according to their demands about looks or the type of function.

He said: "We thought the market would be business people. We have not had much response from Stoke-on-Trent but business is better in more upmarket areas like Newcastle, Stone, Crewe and Nantwich.

"It is amazing how many lonely people there are who feel more secure if they are not on their own.

"These days there are more single women in their 30s and more women getting more senior positions.

"With all the Christmas functions coming up we are getting a lot of inquiries.

"The phone has been going non-stop.

"Clients want someone *who is going* to melt into the background. They might feel uneasy about press-ganging colleagues into going to a function or be lonely."

Karl, who lives with his partner and their son, has been on three jobs to restaurants but prefers to leave the dating game to others.

He said: "It is nerve-wracking being an escort and very similar to going on a blind date.

"Depending on how professional they are the more uneasy I feel because I do not want to be shown up.

"The thing is to make the client feel important. You have to swallow your male ego though by not paying for drinks.

"At the end of the evening I give them a card and thank them."

## Businesswoman Stacy too busy for romance ...

WHEN businesswoman Stacy from Crewe was invited to a function with her firm's clients, she knew what she wanted - a man to look good on the end of her arm.

The 26-year-old has twice booked escorts - for the business do and a family christening - and says: "It is a service just like hiring a suit.

"I have my own business, am very independent and am not looking for any heavy commitment. But I still wanted to maintain an appearance and not feel the odd-one-out at events.

"And it is an ego boost to be seen with an attractive man. I briefed the escort beforehand to say we had been seeing each other for three months.

"It suits me as and when I need it because at the end of the day you can say goodbye.

"If you are a single woman it is easy to pick up idiots - they are two-a-penny - but it is hard to meet decent people. Men are intimidated by women who know what they want. I have male friends I could have taken but I did not want them do it out of pity.

"I prefer not telling people I book escorts because they get the idea you are sad but I have an active social life going out with girlfriends and to the gym."

*Karl the Ice cream man: 'One of my many endeavours before starting an escort business'*

I'll never forget how proud my mother was when her friend—a lonely older gentleman—contacted me in the hope of companionship. For the next few years, he'd take one of my escorts out for dinner twice a month. I witnessed him blossom from someone who was isolated and depressed to a man brimming with charm and excitement. His story is but one of many that still gives me *the buzz*.

That feeling is exactly why I'm here writing this book. I want to share that feeling. I want to share the tried and tested steps that brought me success and inspired the next generation of agencies.

Escorting in the UK is a multi-million-pound industry, and one which I was lucky enough to tap into in 1998. Above all else, it is a business tailored to your expectations. A fledgling agency provides a generous part-time income on the weekends, but anything larger could yield thousands of pounds in revenue every month. At my peak—even as a relatively small, local agency—I had fifty escorts on my books with regular appointments left, right and centre! With the help of this book, you too will be able to do the same. Each chapter features a step-by-step guide for the everyman to establish their own escort agency—with or without the aid of the internet. It contains my approach to branding, advertising and recruitment, managing your operation, working within the law and growing your business into a flourishing enterprise.

Let the buzz begin.

# Escort agencies come out from the shadows

A NORTH Staffordshire businessman has become one of the first escort agency bosses in the country to use jobcentres to recruit workers.

Karl Crossfield, aged 40, set up his business — Karl's Escort Agency — last autumn, advertising for escorts and clients in newspapers and by handing out business cards at nightclubs.

He was looking for people with "an outgoing personality who are easy to get along with". Their duties would include accompanying diners for all occasions, including functions and meals out.

But with the relaxation of the Government's rules, Mr Crossfield turned to jobcentres and widened his search.

Dozens of escorts, who can earn a maximum of £26 an hour, are on his books, both male and female. These include students who turn to the escort industry to ease their growing debt. The agency has male and female escorts but the client base is all-male. His workers are self-employed and pay their own tax and National Insurance.

Mr Crossfield said: "I've had lots of interest from students. They're ideal for me as they have outgoing personalities, are very confident and have great communication skills."

"The nature of the work which is mostly in the mid-

When JACQUELINE GOLD, the brains behind Ann Summers, won a High Court battle to advertise for staff in jobcentres, she called the legal challenge "a fantastic victory for Ann Summers and common sense". JAMIE SUMMERFIELD looks at the implications of the landmark ruling and meets a North Staffordshire entrepreneur who is already exploiting the law change

range, means they can fit it in around their studies. And they're always struggling for money, obviously. They have so much debt these days and now there's tuition fees as well.

"When they get their degrees, many students will not be earning the cash they can earn with the agency while still studying."

Mr Crossfield has pinned up a poster at Keele University Students' Union looking for staff and he is trying the same direct approach at Stafford shire University.

A female university student taken on by the agency after seeing the jobcentre details said: "I'll finish my course in a couple of years owing about £20,000. I have credit and store cards on the go and I was desperate for work. I needed something that was flexible, that I could fit in around my studies.

"I've normally gone for retail

or bar work. When I saw the escort agency on the jobcentre system I thought, 'Hold on a minute. What's going on here.'"

The student, who would not be named, added: "What would it really was the good pay if I spend an evening with a client, I would get paid £45 for five hours' work. Say we went to a restaurant. The client would pay for all the food and drinks. Anything we then did, say a theatre trip, would be paid for by him."

Away from the candlelit meal-for-two or theatre trip, Mr Crossfield accepts that sexual acts may take place between one of his escorts and a client.

He said: "What goes on behind closed doors is strictly between two consenting adults. No escorts are forced into it. My job is to match up clients and escort for an appointment. What goes on between them is strictly up to the escort. All I ask is that if they see a client again it is booked and organised through the agency."

Mr Crossfield says no checks of address or police records are made.

He said: "There is a level of risk involved with setting a client up with an escort but I'm a good judge of character and we've never had any problems of abuse or violence."

Escorts sign a contract with the agency when starting the employment. Part of it states:

"All appointments are made at the escort's own risk and the decision to go ahead with any booking is purely theirs. No responsibility will be accepted by the company whatsoever."

New escorts also sign a declaration when taken on by the agency stating they must never reveal their telephone number or address when seeing a client. "The rule is for your own safety and to maintain your privacy," the declaration says.

Mr Crossfield added: "When a new escort starts I brief them as well as I can on the safety issues. I tell my escorts to always let someone know exactly where they're going

and what time they should be back. If the meeting is taking place at a hotel, escorts should call ahead to see if the client's booked in. Also, I tell them to let the client know that someone's waiting for them at a certain time."

Mr Crossfield added: "Many of my clients are successful, professional people who may not have the time to start a relationship or simply don't want to. Their career is the most important thing to them and they may need an escort for a business function or social event. I drop leaflets at solicitors' offices and accountants.

"But there are also a lot of lonely and shy men out there who need a helping hand to get out and about meeting people.

"At the end of the day I'm providing a service that's very much in demand — and I'm creating new, well paid jobs for people."

Alistair Watson, president of Staffordshire University Students' Union, today expressed disappointment at news students "have to engage in this kind of work to stay afloat".

He added: "I accept that some students may be happy to do this work. But it's a clear sign the Government needs to act urgently to address the issue of student funding."

● Jacqueline Gold

*Me tapping into the escort business at a perfect time*

# 2

## CREATING YOUR AGENCY

Creating any business from scratch is a scary prospect, but rest assured this chapter will guide you through the humble beginnings of your journey. Of course, when I decided to write this book, I decided to write it for the everyday person. I didn't want you—the reader—to have to be an expert web designer or a seasoned entrepreneur with thousands to invest. I established my agency without the internet and very little start-up capital. Twenty-three years later, the very methods I used remain the tried-and-tested backbone of the escorting industry.

Despite this, we must also be aware that 2021 is a little different to 1998. You may well have access to a smartphone or computer, and there's no reason why you can't use these modern tools to help you along the way. This is why I've decided to write this chapter with both aspects in mind.

# Step 1: Create your Business Card

You might be wondering why the first step for creating your escort agency is creating your business card. Surely the first step is to recruit your escorts or prepare your contracts. The answer is simple: It all begins with the card. The card is the first thing many potential clients and escorts will see, and it is, therefore, exactly where you should start. Creating a business card is a lot like putting paint on a canvas for the very first time. It's where you get a feel for the vibe of your business. How do you wish to present it? Who are you targeting? There's no need to write a long-winded business plan to determine this. Sketch out a card and let your agency come to life.

## Choose a name

First and foremost, what are you going to call your agency? My advice is to keep things simple. Karl's Escort Agency was the name of my business. Pretty simple, eh? Those three words alone tell the client who I am and what I do, and from the name alone, they know exactly what they're getting. Of course, you may wish to omit your own name from the business name. In this case, you could use a geographical term to describe the place of operation (such as Herefordshire Escort Agency) or an adjective which signifies the class and sophistication of your operation (such as Diamond Escorts).

## Choose a logo icon for branding purposes

That takes us nicely to the second key aspect of your business card. As I mentioned in the introduction to this book, there is a key distinction between escorting and prostitution. This distinction must be clear on your business card because, whilst it is not illegal to exchange money for sexual services in the UK, it is illegal to own a brothel or to operate a prostitution ring. Therefore, our emphasis must *always* be on social companionship. Your business card should match this. Choose imagery that meets the definition of escorting: social companionship. I personally opted for a silhouette of a man and woman wining and dining. Why? Because it indicates class, and this will be reflected in the services a client receives.

Many of the large independent escorting websites get this side of the business entirely wrong. They advertise page upon page of naked women with every kink, fetish and preference neatly arranged. It's impersonal, unfriendly and leaves nothing to the imagination. It takes away from the excitement of escorting—the flirtatiousness and the adventure—and reduces it down to an exchange of sexual services. More importantly, that's not what well-mannered everyday clients want.

With this in mind, if you have access to a computer, it's very easy to find simple, royalty-free icons. Sites like iconfinder.com offer thousands of options. Programmes like Microsoft Office (Word, PowerPoint, etc.) also come with a great catalogue of icons and have sizing presets for business cards.

## Include key information

It goes without saying that your business card needs to include key information. Other than the name of your business, you'll need to include a contact email and telephone number. My advice is to set up an email account with the name of your business. If you want to keep your personal telephone number private, you could purchase a cheap phone and SIM card for business purposes. Nothing fancy is required here, and the cheapest function-focussed phones on the market often cost less than £50!

Aside from this, it is worth including one or two phrases to catch the eye of the reader. I often opted for:

- Staffordshire, Cheshire and the Moorlands No.1
- All tastes catered for

## Go to print!

A local printing service can take care of this for you, but you can also save money by printing the business cards yourself—as you would any document—on heavy card stock and cutting them out yourself. This is exactly what I did, and the price I paid for a guillotine saved me a lot of money in the long term!

It's also worth noting that you can do all of this without a computer. Simply take your sketch and brief to a local printing service and explain what you're looking for. People often forget that printing agencies have the equipment and expertise on hand to bring your brief and sketch to life. Of course, all this comes at a small price, but once your business card is designed and printed, you've taken that precious first step in establishing your escort agency. As it happens, the business card is also one of the most powerful advertising tools at your disposal—and one of the cheapest.

# Step 2: Understand your Location

You might think that market research is about spending hours upon hours on the internet, conducting polls or researching studies. When it comes to creating a successful escorting agency, however, the reality is far simpler. What we really need is a basic understanding of the location our agency is going to operate in. Who might our clients be, and where might we find them?

## Start with the map

To begin with, pull up a map of your county. Trace your finger around the border and take a deep breath. At the very least, for the first year or two of your operation, these boundaries are where you'll conduct 95 per cent of your business. We'll take Staffordshire as an example for now— seeing as that's where I operated Karl's Escort Agency—

but you can apply these same principles to your county in exactly the same way I discuss them here.

First of all, make a note of the major city (or cities) within your county. In the case of Staffordshire, the largest is Stoke-on-Trent, followed by Lichfield and the market towns of Stafford, Burton-on-Trent and Tamworth. Scattered between are numerous countryside villages. In escorting, there are two primary types of clients: business professionals and regulars. The former will be centred around the cities in your given county, but naturally we need to be more specific than this.

## Drill into the detail

This step becomes much easier with the help of the internet. A few quick and easy steps to find out more about your location and potential client base include:

- Using an interactive map or job sites like Glassdoor. com to find out which national and international businesses are centred in a given area.
- Researching which locations are the most affluent and distinguishing between residential, commercial and cultural areas.
- Making a list of the local hotels using websites like Booking.com to find out which are popular for people on business.
- Getting out on foot and see for yourself where potential clients spend their time. Where are

white-collar professionals eating and drinking on a Friday evening? Which pubs are popular with older gentlemen who might be lonely and in need of company?

## Summarise your findings

Taking Stoke-on-Trent as an example, the steps above provide me with the key information I need to understand my location:

- The area is home to advanced manufacturers such as Jaguar Landrover and Astrazeneca as well as more traditional manufacturers like Michelin and JCB. As it happens, I once provided an escort for an executive at JCB after leaving a brochure at their front desk!
- Business travellers tend to stay in the Hilton DoubleTree or any number of the budget hotels in the Stoke-on-Trent city centre.
- They tend to entertain themselves in the Cultural Quarter.
- The wealthiest residents in the area are situated in Lichfield and Tamworth—both of which are a close commute to both Stoke and Birmingham.

With a few minutes of well-placed research, we already have a rough idea of the areas we'll be targeting for our agency! Advertising is, of course, another matter entirely, but your approach is much the same. You are thinking about those on business in the city who may want a classy companion for a night or two of wining and dining. You are thinking about the wealthy, albeit lonely, individual in an upmarket town who would like a beautiful companion for a wedding or party. These are precisely the clients with whom you'll build a reputation and repeat custom. They are trustworthy, well-paying and well-kept, and they are key to running a successful escorting business.

Of course, you have some choice in the matter. Larger cities make for lucrative opportunities but are likely serviced by a number of pre-existing agencies. Moreover, you might not be interested in the hustle and bustle of running an inner-city enterprise. On the other hand, small towns are often free for the taking in terms of business opportunities, but they rely heavily on the slow-growing repeat custom of regular punters. How you approach your location is entirely up to you, and that's the beauty of the business!

## Step 3: Create a Website (optional)

As I mentioned previously—and contrary to popular belief— the internet might be beneficial to running your agency, but it certainly isn't essential. That said, this guide wouldn't be complete without some quick-fire guidance on how to make the most of technology by creating a website.

One of the best things about internet technology in 2021 is that—for a price—other people will do the majority of the legwork for you. Gone are the days when people like you and I have to spend long nights trying to build websites from scratch. Take for instance HornyDesigns, a company that specifically creates and manages escort agency websites:

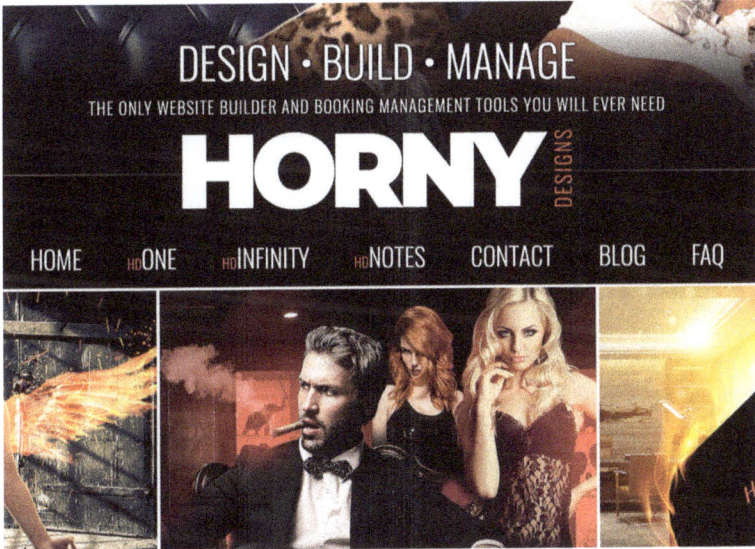

*Screengrab from horneydesings.com*

As you can see, platforms such as HornyDesigns can provide an all-inclusive hub for your operation, including escort profiles, the areas you service, contact details, client screening and management, payment platforms and multiple easy-to-use design tools. Is something like this necessary to get up and running? Absolutely not. Might it be helpful as you expand and grow? Absolutely! One of the most difficult moments in running my own escort agency was when an angry ex-girlfriend threw away my contact records in a fit of rage! Needless to say, the relationship didn't last long after that, but it certainly wouldn't have been a problem if I was able to back up my records on the internet.

With a website in place, you have the added benefit of being able to list your agency on popular escorting platforms, such as Vivastreet.co.uk, which will keep you in good sight of potential clients who are browsing online. Do be wary, however, that these websites typically contain listings for prostitutes—as well as escorts—and the increased visibility may come at the expense of being associated with adult entertainment.

Alternatively, you could create a Facebook page for your business. The Facebook Business Suite includes many features which allow a modern agency to manage its online bookings entirely through the systems built into social media. In my day, I'd have never imagined being able to run a business through a website—let alone social media—but the world has certainly come a long way!

# In Conclusion...

All great enterprises start with a single idea. Here, you've put pen to paper by thinking of your agency name and designing a business card. We focussed on wining and dining and that all important distinction between escorting and prostitution, including the key contact information required to operate.

Next, we explored our local area and started to build an idea of the locations we are going to target and the types of clients available to us. Feeling comfortable and confident in who your services are for is the key to any successful business.

Finally, we considered how a website can be easily created regardless of your technical abilities and can be used to help extend the reach and efficiency of your agency.

At this point, you can give yourself a well-earned congratulations! We might not have any escorts on our books or clients on the phone, but in the most basic sense, we have the framework of your agency in place. I would also recommend registering your business on Gov.uk to make things official. The simplest way to do this is to register as a sole trader, although it's not a legal requirement until you've officially earned more than £1,000 within the tax year. Of course, back in my day, everything was paid in cash, which gave me some leeway with the taxman. In 2021, however, the opposite is true, and many people prefer to pay with instant bank transfers or popular services like PayPal. The last thing you want to do is get caught out for your hard-earned money!

In the next chapter, we'll get our teeth into one of the most important aspects of setting up an escort agency: recruiting your escorts! This is where we will start to see our agency come to life. What could be more exciting than working with a group of sophisticated, beautiful people?

# 3

## RECRUITING YOUR ESCORTS

In this chapter, we will continue the steps in chapter 1 by creating a contract to be used as a basis for the working relationship between you and your escorts. Rest assured, this chapter will show you exactly what kind of contract I used in 1998—expanded and updated for 2021!

We will then discuss the ins and outs of going about recruiting escorts. How are you going to find them? What questions might you ask them? It's certainly an exciting, nerve-wracking step to take, but I'll be here with you at every step!

## Step 4: Write a Contract

A great contract is clear and watertight. It offers protection to both you as the owner of the agency and to the escorts you will be working with. We'll get into this in a little more detail later, but it's important to take each escort through the contract at the interview stage so that any questions, queries or points for negotiation can be agreed upon face-to-face. Although every agency's contract is different, there are a few clauses which must absolutely be included. We will start by discussing each of these in turn.

## The escort is considered an independent contractor.

This clause is the basis for your entire working relationship with the escorts on your books. Being a self-employed contractor, rather than an employee, means that escorts are:

- Not obligated to receive or accept any work from the agency
- Not entitled to typical employee benefits, such as sick pay or a pension plan
- Responsible for declaring their own taxable income to HMRC

It's crucially important that both the agency and the escort understand this clause. The working relationship isn't an offer of employment. There are no guaranteed hours of work. You are simply agreeing to list them as an independent escort through your agency, even if they have never been an escort before. Although this might sound restrictive for the escort, you can remind them of some key benefits:

- The escort can choose their own working hours and their own appointments.

- The escort can work around their existing employment and personal life.
- The escort is not bound to the agency and is free to turn down appointments or terminate the agreement without notice.

This leads us on to our second clause:

## All appointments are arranged and attended at the escort's discretion.

This clause is all about choice and safety. The thinking here is relatively simple:

- It must always be the escort's choice to agree to an arranged appointment.
- It must always be the escort's choice to attend the appointment.
- It must always be at the escort's discretion what happens during the appointment and how long the appointment lasts.

Think about it this way: To operate legally, it must be clear in writing that an escort has never been forced or pressured by you into doing something. It protects you from any false accusations and allows the escort to use their common sense and take charge of their own decisions.

**The agency will arrange the date, time, place and duration of the appointment on behalf of the escort.** Even though it is up to the escort to accept the proposed appointment, the date, time and meeting place must always be pre-arranged by you—the agency. This allows you to:

- Ensure that you know where a working escort is at all times
- Ensure that the fee for the appointment is accurate and correct

Remember, without this clause, there's nothing to stop an escort going into business on their own. What you might've been told is a one-hour appointment could end up being a two-hour appointment, leaving you out of pocket or the escort in an unsafe position. With that said, as an escort builds a network of regular clients, it may be more efficient for them to arrange their own appointments with well-known clients and then communicate these to the agency. This is something which you can treat as a privilege of trust on a case-by-case basis.

**It is the escort's responsibility to collect the agreed payment before commencing the appointment. All monies (less the escort's commission) must be paid to the company at a pre-arranged time (if working on a cash-only basis).**

Alternatively,

**The agency will pay the escort their agreed commission within twenty-four hours of satisfactory completion of the appointment (if working on an electronic payment basis).**

In 1998, cash was king, and it was always the escort's responsibility to collect payment from the client before commencing the appointment. Of course, in 2021, card is king, and your policy may instead be to have each client pay by bank transfer or PayPal before each session. Electronic payments means that you'll never deal with the hassle of a client refusing to pay once an appointment is booked, and you won't have to deal with collecting money from escorts.

**The company will contact each client after the session to ensure that everything was to their satisfaction.**

Having this clause in your contract is a helpful reminder for each escort that—within the confines of consent, safety and autonomy—they are expected to deliver the service of quality companionship for the client. In 1998, I enjoyed telephoning each client after their appointment. It gave me the opportunity to find areas in which to develop and improve the service. Of course, in the vast majority of cases, the client was always thoroughly satisfied, and the phone call doubled as a way to discuss repeat bookings and drum up future business!

**The escort agrees to never share their personal contact information (telephone number, email address or physical address) with a client. All repeat business should be directed through the agency.**

This is a no-brainer and is crucial in terms of protecting both the escort's anonymity and right to a personal life and protecting the business from being undercut at any point.

With this in mind, there are a vast number of clauses you may wish to add to your contract in order to make the agreement between yourself and the escort crystal clear. These vary between agencies but may include:

An agreement on what the escort will be paid per client hour. A typical split is 50/50, which is considered fairly desirable for the agency. However, you should be open to negotiation based on the quality of the applicant. An in-demand escort with several repeat bookings will yield the agency good money in the long-term, even if you have to compromise on the initial split.

An agreement on how the escort will be taken to and from each appointment. I always drove each escort personally, which helped me guarantee both the timeliness and the safety of the booking. As your agency grows, however, you may wish to come to an agreement with a local taxi firm, but this should always be arranged by the agency; you never want to leave an escort waiting around after an appointment has finished.

An agreement on key safety measures. If the escort has a smartphone, they should share their live location with both the agency and a trusted friend for the duration of the appointment. In 2021, there are incredible apps for women's safety, such as Shake2Safety, which triggers an automated message to an emergency contact with subtle movements such as button tapping or phone shaking.

An agreement on how to proceed if the client and escort wish to extend the duration of the session. In this case, the escort should make a quick call to the agency specifying the additional time required and the payment method. The escort may take cash on the spot, or the client could make an instant transfer to the agency. Regardless, contact to the agency should always be made first to ensure safety.

An agreement on how the working agreement should be terminated. Can either party do so without notice or would you prefer additional notice, provided the contract hasn't been violated?

## With exception to the duties outlined above, the agency accepts no responsibility for the independent escort.

This clause should be the final entry in your contract. It's a simple disclaimer that clarifies the limit of your responsibilities.

# KARL`S
# ESCORT AGENCY

ALL APPOINTMENTS ARE MADE AT THE ESCORT`S OWN RISK AND THE DECISION TO GO AHEAD WITH ANY BOOKING IS PURELY THEIRS.

NO RESPONSIBILITY WILL BE ACCEPTED BY THE COMPANY, (KARL`S ESCORT AGENCY) WHATSOEVER.

THE AGENCY WILL ARRANGE THE TIME AND THE DURATION OF ALL APPOINTMENTS, PRIOR TO PASSING THE BOOKING ON TO THE ESCORT, SO THAT THE ESCORT WILL BE ABLE TO ARRIVE AT THE PREARRANGED MEETING POINT BEFORE THE TIME OF THE APPOINTMENT.

IT IS THE ESCORT`S OWN RESPONSIBILITY TO ASK FOR THE AGREED PAYMENT FROM THE CLIENT BEFORE COMMENCING WITH THE APPOINTMENT.

ANY EXTENSION TO THE DURATION OF THE APPOINTMENT WILL BE AT THE DISCRETION OF THE ESCORT AND ALL ADDITIONAL PAYMENTS COLLECTED BEFORE ANY EXTENSION TO THE DURATION.

ALL MONIES (LESS THE ESCORT`S COMMISSION) MUST BE PAID TO THE COMPANY AT A SUITABLE TIME, PREARRANGED BETWEEN THE AGENCY AND THE ESCORT. THIS TIME WILL BE AGREED UPON BEFORE THE ESCORT COLLECTS FROM THE AGENCY THE FULL DETAILS OF THE APPOINTMENT.

IT IS THE COMPANY`S POLICY TO RE-CONTACT ALL CLIENTS AFTERWARDS TO CHECK THAT EVERYTHING WAS TO THE CLIENT`S SATISFACTION.

AT NO TIME SHOULD THE ESCORT EVER GIVE THEIR PHONE NUMBER OR ADDRESS TO THE CLIENT, OR ANY OTHER CONTACT INFORMATION EXCEPT THE AGENCY`S NUMBER.

ALL REPEATED BUSINESS IS TO BE THROUGH THE AGENCY DIRECT FROM THE CLIENT.

ESCORTS ARE ASKED TO REMEMBER AT ALL TIMES THAT THEY ARE A REPRESENTATIVE OF THE AGENCY AND THAT YOUR APPEARANCE AND ATTITUDE WILL BE REFLECTED ON THE IMAGE OF THE AGENCY.

ANY ABUSES TO THE TERMS AND CONDITIONS OF THIS CONTRACT WILL RESULT IN THE TERMINATION OF THE CONTRACT.

Name/Address/Contact Number . . . . . . . . . . . . . . . . . . . . . . . . . . . . . . . . . . . . . . . . . . . . . . . . . . . . . . . . . . . . .

. . . . . . . . . . . . . . . . . . . . . . . . . . . . . . . . . . . . . . . . . . . . . . . . . . . . . . . . . . . . . . . . . . . . . . . . . . . . . . . . . . .

      Escort`s Signature . . . . . . . . . . . . . . . . . . . . .

Signed on and behalf of Karl`s Escort Agency . . . . . . . . . . . . . . . . . . . . . . . . . . . . . . . . . . . . .

# Step 5: Create an Application Process

Although escorting is about charm, sophistication and good company, looks play a huge part. In 1998, my application form asked for information about the prospective escort's hair colour, eye colour and general appearance. In 2021, this may not be necessary; simply requiring applicants to submit a couple of quality unfiltered pictures alongside their application will tell you all that you need to know.

The application process you create will depend largely on the technology you have at your disposal. For example:

- A comprehensive website powered by a pre-existing platform, such as HornyDesigns, provides a simple built-in application form. You can add key questions and photo requests here with ease, which are then all sent directly to your email address.
- If you are managing your business through a Facebook page, you can send and receive photographs and forms directly through Messenger.
- If you are sticking to email only, then application forms can be sent and received upon enquiry.
- If you prefer a physical application, then sending an application form to the prospective escort's postal address with a return envelope included is your best course of action.

Depending on your recruitment strategy (which we'll discuss in the next step), a prospective escort will usually enquire via telephone, email, social media or a website. In either case, try not to have multiple processes for applications; manage them through one platform with a physical option as a backup.

In either case, your application process should include:

1. A job description outlining what an escort is, what an escort does and what an escort's responsibilities are.

2. An application form in which to include:
   - Key contact information
   - Descriptive characteristics, such as height, age and ethnicity. Never ask for anything too personal such as waist, bust or build.
   - Space to describe previous or relevant experience
   - Space to describe why the applicant wants to be an escort and work with the agency
   - Availability
   - Preferences

3. A request for two or three photographs of the applicant. Images featuring full or partial nudity are not permitted. Opt for unfiltered everyday photos: one of the face and one full-body.

# Step 6: Begin a Recruitment Strategy

In many ways, recruitment goes hand-in-hand with advertising, which we will discuss in the next chapter. For every prospective client who hears about your agency and sees a flyer, post or business card, so too will a prospective escort.

To put it simply, recruitment is all about having an entrepreneurial spirit. Putting yourself and your agency out there for the very first time is a nerve-wracking experience. What will people think? What if people judge? What if there is a backlash, or what if I receive no applications? I felt all those worries myself back in 1998, and no doubt if I was to start all over, I'd feel them today!

Entrepreneurial spirit goes a long way here, but so does knowledge. Be assured in the knowledge that escorting is perfectly legal. Be assured in the knowledge that escorting is safe, above-board and can provide a meaningful, unforgettable service. You're going to make people happy, and although escorting isn't for everyone, you are going to help many talented individuals establish a great source of income.

Also keep in mind that escorts should never be charged a fee for joining the agency. This is part of what makes working with you appealing; there is no financial risk for the independent escort.

The following strategies should be your primary avenues of direct recruitment:

- A version of your flyer or business card amended for 'escorts wanted'. You can then hand these out or post them up around nightclubs, bars and entertainment hotspots.
- Students' unions at nearby universities. Many will allow advertisements for escort agencies. I recruited heavily from Keele University in the early 2000s and never encountered any issues.
- Various job sites geared towards escorts, such as Vivastreet and Red-Life. Do be wary, however, that these also include vacancies for erotic entertainment and prostitution.
- Open recruitment via your website or social media page.

In 1998, I was one of the first escort agencies to advertise directly at the jobcentre. At the time, this was supported by a 2003 ruling brought about by Jacqueline Gold—the CEO of Anne Summers—which clarified that the lawful adult sector had the right to advertise vacancies through the job centre. Nowadays, however, internal policies have tightened, and openings in the adult sector are only permitted as jobcentre listings for retail (such as sex toys and lingerie) rather than the provision of services (such as escorting). In terms of mainstream recruitment, this is perhaps our most frustrating hurdle: dismissing escort vacancies on the incorrect assumption that they are of a sexual nature.

Although you are bound to encounter this kind of pushback, simply explaining the nature of your business in detail goes a long way. More importantly, these limitations are more than compensated by the limitless recruitment opportunities available through the internet.

## Step 7: Interview Prospective Applicants

Once applications start arriving through your chosen recruitment platforms, it's entirely up to you how you identify prospective escorts. With this in mind, there are a few approaches that served me well in practice:

- Most clients are men seeking women, so aim for an 80/20 or 90/10 split between female and male escorts.
- It's worth having a dozen or so escorts on your books before you start trading; remember that their appeal and availability will vary. Parties and nights out generally call for someone who is young, good-looking and glamorous. Dinner dates require someone who is a good match for the client in terms of personality and their ability to make them feel at ease. Functions and events typically require an escort to be sophisticated, charming and 'play a role'.

This is exactly why you must interview every prospective escort who passes your initial application with careful consideration to:

- Conduct the interview in a public place for safety purposes, such as a coffee shop or quiet restaurant.
- Dress professionally; remember that you are representing the agency from the word 'go', and perception is king.
- Bring all relevant paperwork; a successful interview will conclude with a contract signing, which you should always be prepared for.

Finally, during the interview, you should keep the following questions in mind:

- Is the applicant well-dressed and well-kempt with good personal hygiene?
- Is the applicant charming, polite and well-spoken? Do you feel at ease in their company?
- Is the applicant enthusiastic about working as an escort? What are their reasons for wanting to work with the agency?
- Does the applicant have a clear understanding of what an escort is and what the agency's policies and expectations are?
- Does the applicant have any preferences or prejudices regarding the types of clients they would be happy to meet?

- Could the applicant adapt to the expectations of differing clients? Are they happy to play the role of the girlfriend/boyfriend, the elegant plus-one or the companion at a large event or function?
- Does the applicant drink alcohol? Do they feel comfortable and responsible working in an environment where alcohol may be present, such as a night out or dinner date?

I found that the best escorts were—above all else—adaptable. They were completely at home being themselves yet perfectly able to play whatever role the client and event called for. They were happy to dress up, dress down or dress as someone entirely different if the occasion called for it. I even kept a supply of wigs so that escorts could have whatever hair colour the client wished!

Provided you're happy with an applicant, the final step is to agree on a rate and sign on the dotted line. As I mentioned previously, the desired split is 50/50 per client hour between the agency and escort. However, this should always be open to negotiation. We will discuss more on specific pricing policies in chapter 4.

## In Conclusion...

Recruiting your first pool of escorts is perhaps one of the most exciting and nerve-wracking aspects of setting up your agency. However, once the ball is rolling, it's difficult to stop! Within seven weeks of setting up my own agency in 1998, I had almost thirty escorts on my books, which was more than enough to get started.

As your business grows, recruitment becomes a gradual, ongoing progress which requires less and less direct effort. Enquiries will come directly to your inbox as a result of advertising and word-of-mouth. Happy escorts will often refer their friends to the agency for work, and over time, your pool will quickly grow.

Finally, always remember to store information about your escorts in a locked file or password-protected computer. You should also create an online backup using a service like Google Drive. I'll never forget the day an angry ex-girlfriend threw away my folder in a fit of rage! She practically destroyed my agency overnight—something which would've never happened had I backed everything up.

In the next chapter, we'll start taking your established agency out into the world by determining a comprehensive advertising strategy and drumming up some business!

# 4

## ADVERTISING YOUR BUSINESS

n this chapter, we will continue the steps outlined in the previous two chapters by taking our concept and services to market. Much like recruitment, advertising is an ongoing strategy with dozens of potential avenues. Naturally, you will adapt these to the given market as discussed in chapter 1.

## Step 8: Finalise Your Pricing

Your promotional material will usually include pricing information. Although you probably have a good idea at this point what your rates will be, now is the time to finalise them.

- Start by researching local escort agencies and finding out their price points. Ignore the agencies that are clearly a thinly veiled prostitution ring and look for key terms such as 'wining and dining' or 'social companionship'.

- Determine a pricing policy based on an hourly rate. Remember that an escort charges for their time, not their services. The service is simply their company; everything else is up to the imagination.
- If you are solely targeting business professionals, high-class clients or affluent areas, scale your prices up accordingly. The same applies if you have been very selective in your recruitment and are seeking to provide top-tier escorts.
- 

A sample pricing policy for a regular agency in line with the current market might appear as follows:

| 1 hour | £100 |
|--------|------|
| 2 hours | £175 |
| 3 hours | £230 |
| All night | £600 |

As you can imagine, these prices are what makes escorting such a lucrative game. My own escort agency gave many university students a fantastic income throughout their studies. If the choice was between bar work for minimum wage or £100 for an evening of dinner and drinks, the choice was a no brainer! As a matter of fact, many students wanted to continue working for the agency after they graduated. All of this makes for an important part of the ongoing recruitment pitch.

# KARL`S ESCORT AGENCY

## ESCORT PRICES

Wining and Dining / Functions etc,.

1 Hr - £40

2 Hr - £65

3 Hr - £80

Up to 6 Hrs - £90

(All day or evening e.g. Wedding up to 6 hrs max.)

-- Split 50/50
Escort and Agency

## Services Optional

| Staffordshire | | | Cheshire | | |
|---|---|---|---|---|---|
| | Escort | Agency | | Escort | Agency |
| 1 hr - £80 | £50 | £30 | 1 hr - £100 | £60 | £40 |
| 2 hr - £125 | £80 | £45 | 2 hr - £145 | £95 | £50 |
| All night - £200 | £125 | £75 | All night - £250 | £150 | £100 |

# Step 9: Create Physical Promotional Material

Your physical promotional material will largely consist of business cards and flyers (A4/A5). Creating a flyer can be approached in much the same way as we used to create our business card in chapter 1. For example:

- Sketching your design and brief and taking them to a local printers
- Designing material yourself on applications such as Microsoft Word or Adobe Indesign
- Using an external agency to create a flyer according to your written brief

# KARL`S
# ESCORT AGENCY

## ESCORT PROFILE

NAME ................................................ AGE ...................

BUILD & STATISTICS ...............................................

EYE COLOUR ..................... HAIR COLOUR ...............

LOOKS ...............................................................

PERSONALITY ......................................................

INTERESTS/HOBBIES ............................................
.........................................................................

████████████ ] ... GAY [ ] ... BI [ ] ... STRAIGHT [ ] ...

AVAILABILITY: DAYS .................... NIGHTS ...............

TIMES ...............................................................

CONTACT NUMBERS: ..........................................

ADDRESS ...........................................................
.........................................................................

DISTANCE PREPARED TO TRAVEL ..........................

DO YOU HAVE YOUR OWN TRANSPORT ...................

ANY PREJUDICES ................................................

**ALL INFORMATION IS STRICTLY CONFIDENTIAL**
ALL INFORMATION HEREIN IS STRICTLY PRIVATE AND CONFIDENTIAL AND WILL ONLY
BE USED BY THE AGENCY TO OBTAIN BOOKINGS FOR YOURSELF.
YOUR ADDRESS AND TELEPHONE NUMBER ARE FOR OUR USE ONLY AND ARE NEVER
PASSED ON TO CLIENTS

# KARL`S
# ESCORT AGENCY

ALL APPOINTMENTS ARE MADE AT THE ESCORT`S OWN RISK AND THE DECISION TO GO AHEAD WITH ANY BOOKING IS PURELY THEIRS.

NO RESPONSIBILITY WILL BE ACCEPTED BY THE COMPANY, (KARL`S ESCORT AGENCY) WHATSOEVER.

THE AGENCY WILL ARRANGE THE TIME AND THE DURATION OF ALL APPOINTMENTS, PRIOR TO PASSING THE BOOKING ON TO THE ESCORT, SO THAT THE ESCORT WILL BE ABLE TO ARRIVE AT THE PREARRANGED MEETING POINT BEFORE THE TIME OF THE APPOINTMENT.

IT IS THE ESCORT`S OWN RESPONSIBILITY TO ASK FOR THE AGREED PAYMENT FROM THE CLIENT BEFORE COMMENCING WITH THE APPOINTMENT.

ANY EXTENSION TO THE DURATION OF THE APPOINTMENT WILL BE AT THE DISCRETION OF THE ESCORT AND ALL ADDITIONAL PAYMENTS COLLECTED BEFORE ANY EXTENSION TO THE DURATION.

ALL MONIES (LESS THE ESCORT`S COMMISSION) MUST BE PAID TO THE COMPANY AT A SUITABLE TIME, PREARRANGED BETWEEN THE AGENCY AND THE ESCORT. THIS TIME WILL BE AGREED UPON BEFORE THE ESCORT COLLECTS FROM THE AGENCY THE FULL DETAILS OF THE APPOINTMENT.

IT IS THE COMPANY`S POLICY TO RE-CONTACT ALL CLIENTS AFTERWARDS TO CHECK THAT EVERYTHING WAS TO THE CLIENT`S SATISFACTION.

AT NO TIME SHOULD THE ESCORT EVER GIVE THEIR PHONE NUMBER OR ADDRESS TO THE CLIENT, OR ANY OTHER CONTACT INFORMATION EXCEPT THE AGENCY`S NUMBER.

ALL REPEATED BUSINESS IS TO BE THROUGH THE AGENCY DIRECT FROM THE CLIENT.

ESCORTS ARE ASKED TO REMEMBER AT ALL TIMES THAT THEY ARE A REPRESENTATIVE OF THE AGENCY AND THAT YOUR APPEARANCE AND ATTITUDE WILL BE REFLECTED ON THE IMAGE OF THE AGENCY.

ANY ABUSES TO THE TERMS AND CONDITIONS OF THIS CONTRACT WILL RESULT IN THE TERMINATION OF THE CONTRACT.

Name/Address/Contact Number . . . . . . . . . . . . . . . . . . . . . . . . . . . . . . . . . . . . . . . . . . . . . . . . . . . . . . . . . . . . . . . . . . . .

. . . . . . . . . . . . . . . . . . . . . . . . . . . . . . . . . . . . . . . . . . . . . . . . . . . . . . . . . . . . . . . . . . . . . . . . . . . . . . . . . . . . .

Escort`s Signature . . . . . . . . . . . . . . . . . . . . . . .

Signed on and behalf of Karl`s Escort Agency . . . . . . . . . . . . . . . . . . . . . . . . . . . . . . . . . . . . . . . .

# Staffordshire`s & Cheshire`s No.1

## KARL`S ESCORT AGENCY

**All escorts are self-employed and responsible for their own tax and insurance.**

Signed . . . . . . . . . . . . . . . . . . . .

Name . . . . . . . . . . . . . . . . . . . .

# KARL`S
# ESCORT AGENCY
## VERY IMPORTANT

The escort at all times should never reveal their telephone number or their address when contacting a client, even repeat bookings will be via the Agency. This rule is for your own safety and to maintain your privacy.

Anyone found breaking this rule, will no longer be employed by the Agency.

Please abide by this condition at all times.

Signed on behalf of the Agency ....................

Signature of Escort .........................

Dated this Day ..............................

.Every agency's flyer—depending on who their targeting—will look different, but they typically include common phrases such as:

- Social companionship
- Private, discreet and confidential
- All tastes catered for
- Business, charity functions and events

In my own material, I always wanted the prospective client to feel like I was talking directly to them. Every agency is unique, but a friendly tone was the key to my success. In any case, the flyer may also feature an 'About Us' section, which can be used to briefly describe your specialties and expertise; don't be afraid to big up your business!

Finally, the flyer should conclude with the relevant information required to make a booking, such as:

- Key contact information and the hours during which your telephone line is open
- Basic information about pricing and payment
- Any relevant discounts (such as a 10% off code on the flyer or a first booking discount)

# Step 10: Distribute Physical Material

Business cards, leaflets and flyers collectively make for the cheapest form of direct advertising. Distributing free printed material is perfectly legal when placed:

- Through a letterbox
- Inside a building, bus or taxi

Other forms of leafleting may be restricted by local bylaws under the Clean Neighbourhoods and Environment Act 2005. The following strategies typically require a permit from the local council:

- Hand-to-hand leafleting
- Placing leaflets on public notice boards
- Placing leaflets on cars parked in a public space or car park
- Placing leaflets in public toilets or other council-owned facilities

With this in mind, your distribution strategy can come to life. Advertising became second nature to me in 1998, and I never went anywhere without a stack of business cards and leaflets. From the get-go, I'd approach the reception desks of businesses and hotels and politely ask if I could leave some leaflets. You'd be surprised how far you can get by being well presented and courteous, and 95% of the time, I was permitted to leave a few leaflets with the receptionist.

I approached every outlet from big offices to bars, pubs and takeaways, and I successfully distributed thousands of leaflets and business cards over the years. That's what the entrepreneurial spirit is all about. You're bound to have a few funny looks or rejections here and there, but does it really matter? Do we really care? When it really comes down to it, the answer is no. We care about making money and making people happy in the confidence that we are providing an ethical and legal service.

## Step 11: Create a Digital Marketing Strategy

As we've previously discussed, the internet is by no means a necessary tool for setting up your agency, but it can be incredibly helpful. In 2021, many clients come across escort agencies directly through the internet, and a digital strategy will help you tap into this market. Some approaches include:

- Posting content on relevant Facebook community pages
- Using Google Ads to ensure that your website is a top hit when users search relevant terms, such as "Stoke-on-Trent escorts"

- Joining a recognised association, such as the UK National Escort Association (UKNEA), and listing your business on their website
- Listing your agency on one of the many escorting directories, such as Vivastreet

## Step 12: Advertise in the Local Newspaper

Although this comes at a greater cost, advertising in the local newspaper is a tried and tested way to drum up business for your agency. In 1998, I established a weekly arrangement with the *Staffordshire Advertiser*. Classy escort agencies focusing on the wining and dining have the added benefit of standing out amidst the usual mix of massage parlours and call girls.

Another way to advertise your agency is by providing stories directly to the newspaper. I would regularly provide interesting, free stories to *The Sentinel*. Escorting is an exciting industry which the press love to swarm around, and you should always be ready to take advantage of this!

# In Conclusion...

There are dozens of ways for a prospective agency to get the word out and start creating business. Some are free and some are expensive. Some require a technical know-how, and others simply require a printer! Defining your own advertisement strategy will come down to your individual skill and style. Some agency owners, like myself, are more than happy to be the face of the business. I embraced telling people about my enterprise, handing out leaflets and being featured in the local paper. Others may feel a little more shy, in which case advertising over the internet or using a distribution agency is going to work best.

Regardless of your approach, the bottom line is well established. There are thousands of people who are longing for some quality companionship and are happy to pay for it. There are countless professionals who want an eye-catching date for an event, night out or evening at the casino. All you need to do is give them a chance to hear about your business and let the magic happen.

# 5

## OPERATING YOUR AGENCY

When the first email lands in your inbox, the phone rings for the first time or an online enquiry arrives, you will certainly feel *the buzz*. It is the moment you've been waiting for: the moment your business begins to function and all your hard work cumulates. With that said, it is a moment you absolutely must be prepared for. Ensuring that your operations are smooth and, above all else, safe is what makes for the success of an agency. This chapter has been designed with that very first phone call in mind, preparing you to be ahead of the game and ready to operate.

## Step 13: Understand the Law

Before getting started, it is important to understand the law as it currently applies to both escorting and prostitution. Even though you're only dealing with the former, understanding how the law applies to the latter will prevent you from

slipping up. The Sexual Offences Act 2003 clarifies that:
- The exchange of sexual services for money is legal.
- Soliciting for the selling of sexual services, or 'kerb crawling', is illegal.
- Owning or managing a brothel is illegal.
- Controlling the exchange of sexual services of another individual is illegal.

This last point is perhaps the most important for you to remember. It is precisely why your branding and advertising makes no mention of sex, even though an independent escort may choose to have sex with a client. With this in mind:
- If a client mentions anything of a sexual nature when contacting the agency, ask them to refer to the independent escort's external profile (such as a Vivastreet profile), and clarify that this is something which can only be discussed with the escort.
- If an escort asks any questions relating to the exchange of sexual services, clarify that this is an independent decision at their discretion and unrelated to the service the agency provides, which is setting up the appointment.

# Step 14: Ensure All Relevant Safety Procedures are in Place

Although this will be partly discussed when contracting an escort, it is important to have a detailed set of safety procedures in place before any bookings take place. This is perhaps the most important step within this entire guide and should never be overlooked. As an agency, it is your ethical responsibility to consider the following safety procedures:

- Providing information on how to stay protected from drink spiking and the key signs to look out for, such as an unusually cloudy, frothy or foamy drink. The escort should also be aware of the early symptoms of drink spiking, including drowsiness, nausea and light-headedness. Several freely available handouts can be found online

- An awareness of drink spiking goes hand-in-hand with alcohol safety. All escorts should commit to staying aware and staying within their limits in order to keep a clear perception of the situation.

- Ensuring that all escorts have access to protection in the event of consensual relations between the escort and client.

- Ensuring that all escorts are committed to sharing the details of each booking with a close friend or partner.

- Ensuring that escorts enable live location tracking for the duration of the appointment via their smartphone and install any relevant safety applications. Escorts should keep their mobile phones charged and on-hand at all times and register the emergency services on speed-dial.

- Ensuring that any extension to an appointment is requested directly from the escort to the agency via telephone.

- Ensuring that the escort agrees to withhold personally identifiable information from their clients, including their address, telephone number, surname and social media channels.

- Ensuring that each client is screened for their name, address and telephone number prior to the appointment being arranged. If they are staying in a hotel, ask for their room number and call them back discreetly via the front desk to confirm their location.

- Ensuring that each client sounds well-mannered, politely-spoken and unintoxicated when speaking over the phone.

- Ensuring that the escort telephones the client prior to the booking in order to inform their own autonomous decision.

- Ensuring that bookings for restaurants, bars, nightclubs and functions are taking place at legitimate, established locations.

- Ensuring that travel arrangements are made and agreed prior to the appointment taking place. Always opt to drive an escort to and from the appointment yourself, use a close friend or pre-book a trustworthy taxi company.

- Signing up for the Ugly Mugs Scheme (nationaluglymugs.org), a free database listing thousands of previously identified 'risky punters'.

Although this list isn't comprehensive, it contains the solid foundations necessary to define your own safety procedures. It might feel a little overwhelming, but knowing that you've done your utmost to keep your escorts safe provides the peace of mind necessary to operate. Moreover, in 2021, safety is becoming an increasingly relevant part of the branding of your operation. Job sites, student unions and newspapers are often proud—rather than hesitant—to support agencies which feature cutting-edge safety standards. In any case, there are more benefits to safety procedures than risk mitigation alone.

## Step 15: Finalise Your Booking Procedure

Naturally, this varies depending on where your enquiries come from. A good booking procedure will seamlessly integrate your agency's safety procedures without unnecessarily burdening the client. A typical booking process might operate as follows:

1. The client contacts the agency via telephone, email, a messenger application or a website booking form.
2. The client is screened for key contact information and provides booking information, including the date, time and duration; the details of the location and event; and what kind of escort and companion they are hoping for. Pricing is confirmed.

Note that if the client makes any mention of sexual services, clarify that this is not something that the agency can discuss for legal reasons; it can only be discussed with the escort.

3. Conduct any further screening required as per your safety procedures and the nature of the booking.
4. After the initial phone call or online exchange, offer the appointment to an appropriate escort, who can then telephone the client directly in order to discuss the details of the booking and decide whether to accept the appointment.
5. Payment information (such as an account number or PayPal link) can be provided directly over the telephone by the escort or via email by the agency. If you are choosing to operate in cash, the client should be made aware that the escort will need to be paid prior to the appointment commencing.
6. Arrange transport for the escort to and from the appointment, once again ensuring that personal safety procedures are understood and followed

before, during and after the appointment.

7.  After the appointment, contact the client at an appropriate time to ensure that the booking was to their satisfaction. Keep this discussion light; you aren't looking for any details, just a green light.

8.  Transfer the escort their agreed fee. If the escort has collected cash, arrange to collect the agency's fee in an appropriate and timely manner.

Although I've spelled out this process in black and white, in practice, these steps are far more colourful. I remember telephoning one escort—a fantastic young lady—following her appointment one evening. To my surprise, she was ecstatic.

"Karl!" she gasped, "That was brilliant. You've got to get me another booking with him again!"

"Oh?" I replied, "It was only a hotel booking. Did something exciting happen?"

As it happened, it was the easiest £100 she'd ever made. The client wanted nothing more than to walk around on all fours for two hours, fully clothed, while being spanked and barking like a dog! Rest assured, there's never a dull day in the world of escorting.

# Step 16: Managing your Escorts

The escorts on your books are the bread and butter of your business. They should feel supported by your agency and confident in the knowledge that you will be able to provide them with consistent, reliable and safe work. Although it will quickly become clear who your most active, hard-working escorts are, it can quickly become overwhelming trying to keep track of everyone and keep everyone happy.

At any given time, I usually had fifty active escorts on my books, and as your business grows, you too will need a way to quickly sift through the pile whenever a client comes calling. Typically, you will choose to store escort information in either:

- A physical folder or binder
- A digital database on your computer or in the cloud (such as Google Drive)

In any case, you should have an entry for each escort containing key information, including:

- The escort's profile and contact information
- Photographs of the escort
- Their agreed rate/split and transport preferences
- A record of their past bookings and repeat clients
- Any noteworthy information, such as preferences and prejudices

It is also vital that escorts feel appreciated and cared for by the agency. This fosters trust and loyalty between both parties. Best practice for working well with your escorts includes:

- Having clear and well thought out safety procedures as discussed in Step 14
- Being careful not to over-manage your escorts or require excessive communication; a sense of independence is key
- Providing financial incentives in return for hard-working escorts, such as a better rate/split
- Being easily available via text or phone in order to promptly answer any concerns or queries they have
- Keeping the confidentiality of individual escorts protected; avoid group chats or large email threads
- Doing your best to treat all escorts equally and fairly

# Step 17: Preparing for Peak Hours

It is always best practice to require a 24-hour notice prior to any booking taking place. However, once your agency has a foothold, Friday and Saturday nights inevitably come with requests for on-the-night bookings. In order to prepare for this, you could:

- Have a small list of escorts who are willing to be on call during peak hours. It's important that these escorts live close by.

• Spend Friday and Saturday evenings with a couple of on-call escorts at a local pub or bar. This will allow you to take them directly to bookings as they come in.

My preference was to always book a quiet table at my local pub on a Friday and Saturday evening for myself and my 'favourite' escort at the time. I was never drinking—as I was the designated driver—but the escort could have whatever she pleased. Inevitably, within an hour or two, the phone would ring, and I'd take her straight to and from an on-the-night booking. Often by the time she'd finished one appointment, another would already be waiting!

Obviously, being on call will usually warrant a more favourable split for the escort as well as any food or drinks you purchase on the night. However, being able to capitalise on on-the-night bookings can be an incredibly lucrative way to spend a weekend evening, provided you don't already have plans!

## Step 18: Managing your Finances

As with any business, it is important to manage your finances. The best way of doing this is to create a sheet detailing both the income and cost to the agency. You will incur costs related to:

• The revenue split of each appointment with the escort

- The fuel and transport costs to and from each appointment
- Any relevant safety procedures and applications
- Refreshments and drinks for the escorts, particularly for on-the-night bookings
- The printing and design of business cards and flyers
- Newspaper advertisements
- Online advertisements and listings

Perhaps the biggest appeal of running an escort agency in terms of cost is that it comes with virtually zero overheads. You don't need to rent an office or building. You don't need to purchase any particular equipment. Aside from advertising and safety measures, the costs you incur will simply scale with your income. Because escorting is legal, don't forget that it is taxable! Keep all your receipts and make sure to register before you're up and running.

The big question on everyone's mind is usually, How much will I make? That's a tricky question to answer because it ultimately comes down to your legwork and your aims. Is your escort agency about creating a small, quiet side hustle targeting a weekend market? Or are you aiming to make this a full-time job and a route to riches? In every sense the choice is yours, but I will try to give a clearer idea in the next step!

# Step 19: Growing your Agency

A small, part-time operation geared towards a small market might involve fifteen or so escorts across an average of five bookings per week. This could generate anywhere between £1,500 and £3,000 in monthly revenue.

A part-time operation with a more established pool of repeat and on-the-night bookings might involve thirty or so escorts across ten to fifteen bookings per week. This could generate anywhere between £4,000 and £8,000 in monthly revenue.

You can, therefore, see the incentive of running a full-time operation. This might involve fifty or more escorts across an average of twenty bookings per week. This could generate anywhere between £6,000 and £12,000 in monthly revenue.

Building your business ultimately comes down to revisiting the steps we have previously discussed in this book through a process of:

- Comprehensive, high-quality advertising
- Providing a safe, seamless and valuable service to cultivate a great reputation and repeat bookings
- Attracting and recruiting the highest quality escorts suitable for your individual agency

Although we initially discussed these steps in terms of an entry-level, low-budget operation, as your business scales up, it is important to invest in order to keep the quality high and the business smooth! For example:

- Consider recruiting an administrative assistant to help with bookings, recruitment and record-keeping.
- Consider hiring a webmaster to manage, operate and update your website.
- Contract designers to create high-quality branding and advertising materials.
- When targeting new markets, consider bringing a 'franchisee' on board—someone to set up a wing of your agency in another location in return for a predetermined revenue split.
- Consider collaborating with professional organisations such as MASH or the UKNEA in order to improve brand perception and reputation.

It's worth mentioning that you yourself may, at times, choose to work as an escort for the agency. Perhaps an enquiry comes in for a simple dinner date, and you realise that you tick every box!

This is something I was fortunate enough to enjoy myself from time to time, and it must be said that getting closer to the action is a great way to see how well your agency is *really* operating. In any case, being an escort follows much of the same advice we already covered. Safety comes first, and you are a self-employed individual, responsible for your own insurance and tax.

# In Conclusion...

Ensuring that you work both safely and legally is perhaps the most important aspect of running an escort agency. Once you have got those two boxes ticked, there is nothing left to do except focus on growing your agency into a bustling, profitable enterprise! Of course, every agency is different, but the steps in this chapter are of crucial importance; they are the difference between legal, ethical and operational success or the story of yet another agency who have failed their escorts and failed their clients.

Of course, I say this with a smile on my face because the information here contains everything you need to know in order to avoid these pitfalls!

# 6

## FINAL THOUGHTS

The good company of beautiful people. The sound of a happy client. The money I deposited into my account each week. For all the jobs I have had over the years, nothing comes close to the magic of running my own escort agency.

Perhaps the most exciting part of writing this book has been the chance to revisit and relive some of those feelings which I experienced time and time again over the past twenty years. Naturally, you might be asking yourself, Karl, why write a book? Why not just get back in the game!

The truth is that I would get back in the game—following the exact process I laid out in this book—if I was ten years younger! As it happens, this book is more like a retirement gift from the old veteran to you: the escort agency of the future.

These days, I am more than happy operating my tractor train in Staffordshire and Cheshire, giving back to

For hire in Staffordshire & Cheshire

Novelty fun ride

For all the family

# TRACTOR TRAIN
## FOR ALL YOUR EVENTS & PRIVATE PARTIES

- Open to kids & adults of all ages, our novelty fun ride is made for all events.
- Able to carry upto 30 children and can be utilised for any type of occasion
- Available for events in and around Staffordshire & Cheshire, such as Spring Fayre's, Summer Fete's and more
- Tailor measured for any occasion as it is not fixed on a railway line
- Negotiable fee for private parties
- £1 per person if booked by a private organisation. (A donation will be given at the end of the day)

For more information or to discuss a booking please call Karl on 07789 300539

More information available online

# WWW.TRACTORTRAIN.CO.UK

the community and seeing the happy faces of parents and children as I take them around.

In truth, my health isn't what it used to be either, and I am currently awaiting open-heart surgery. I'm not entirely sure if I could take the excitement of operating an escort agency nowadays!

It should, therefore, be no surprise to hear that I am more than happy to be living a semi-retired life. Writing this book is all about passing on my knowledge. Of course, the hard work is down to you, and I want to stress that none of what I've written here is a guarantee of success. What I can promise, however, is that the steps we've discussed are a comprehensive foundation upon which you could certainly build a flourishing escort agency.

That prospect is, after all, what the entrepreneurial spirit is all about. The thrill and the chase; the risk and reward; and above all else...*the buzz!*